A Note to Parents

DK READERS is a compelling program for beginning readers, designed in conjunction with leading literacy experts, including Dr. Linda Gambrell, Professor of Education at Clemson University. Dr. Gambrell has served as President of the National Reading Conference and the College Reading Association, and has recently been elected to serve as President of the International Reading Association.

Beautiful illustrations and superb full-color photographs combine with engaging, easy-to-read stories to offer a fresh approach to each subject in the series. Each DK READER is guaranteed to capture a child's interest while developing his or her reading skills, general knowledge, and love of reading.

The five levels of DK READERS are aimed at different reading abilities, enabling you to choose the books that are exactly right for your child:

Pre-level 1: Learning to read
Level 1: Beginning to read
Level 2: Beginning to read alone
Level 3: Reading alone
Level 4: Proficient readers

The "normal" age at which a child begins to read can be anywhere from three to eight years old. Adult participation through the lower levels is very helpful for providing encouragement, discussing storylines, and sounding out unfamiliar words.

No matter which level you select, you can be sure that you are helping your child learn to read, then read to learn!

Penguin Random House

For Dorling Kindersley
Senior Editor Laura Gilbert
Managing Art Editor Ron Stobbart
Publishing Manager Catherine Saunders
Art Director Lisa Lanzarini
Associate Publisher Simon Beecroft
Category Publisher Alex Allan
Production Editor Sean Daly
Production Controller Rita Sinha
Reading Consultant Dr. Linda Gambrell

For Lucasfilm
Executive Editor J. W. Rinzler
Art Director Troy Alders
Keeper of the Holocron Leland Chee
Director of Publishing Carol Roeder

Designed and edited by Tall Tree Ltd
Designer Sandra Perry
Editor Jon Richards

First published in the United States in 2011
by DK Publishing
345 Hudson Street, New York, New York 10014

15 10 9 8 7

DK books are available at special discounts when purchased in bulk
for sales promotions, premiums, fund-raising, or educational use.
For details, contact:
DK Publishing Special Markets
345 Hudson Street
New York, New York 10014
SpecialSales@dk.com

A catalog record for this book is available
from the Library of Congress.

ISBN: 978-0-7566-8279-8 (Paperback)
ISBN: 978-0-7566-8278-1 (Hardback)

Reproduced by Media Development and Printing Ltd., UK
Printed in China

www.starwars.com
www.dk.com

A WORLD OF IDEAS:
SEE ALL THERE IS TO KNOW

Contents

DK READERS

LEARNING
pre-level
1
TO READ

STAR WARS

THE CLONE WARS ™

Don't Wake the Zillo Beast!

Jon Richards

Watch your step!
Some creatures are
friendly.
Other creatures are
dangerous.

Zillo (ZIL-LOH) Beast

Look at this enormous Zillo Beast. He has very sharp teeth.

teeth

Look at these
hungry gutkurrs.

gutkurrs (GUT-CURS)

spikes

They have spikes
on their backs.

Look at this kwazel maw.
It has colorful marks
on its body.

marks

kwazel maw (KWAY-ZELL MOR)

leg

Look at this
Rishi eel.

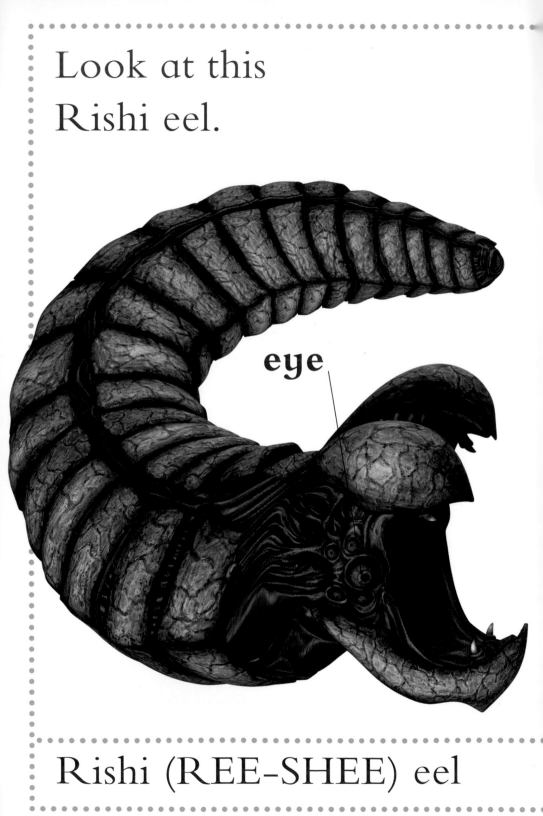

eye

Rishi (REE-SHEE) eel

It lives inside dark holes
on a cold moon.

Look at this angry gundark.
It has four very strong arms.

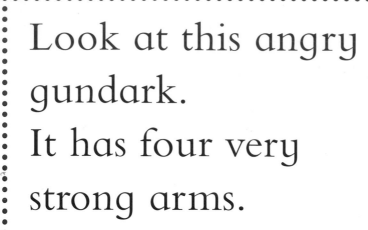

large ears

arms

trooper

skalder (SKOLL-DER)

Look at this
huge skalder.
It has very
thick skin.

thick skin

Look at
this mastiff
phalone.

beak

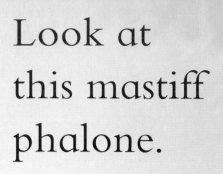

mastiff phalone
(MASS-TIFF FAA-LOAN)

It has a sharp, pointed beak.

ice

narglatch (NAR-GLATCH)

Look at this spiky
narglatch.
It lives on an icy moon.

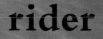

rider

Look at these
peaceful shaaks.

shaaks (SHOCKS)

They live in groups
called herds.

Look at this flying xandu. It flaps its powerful wings.

xandu (ZAN-DOO)

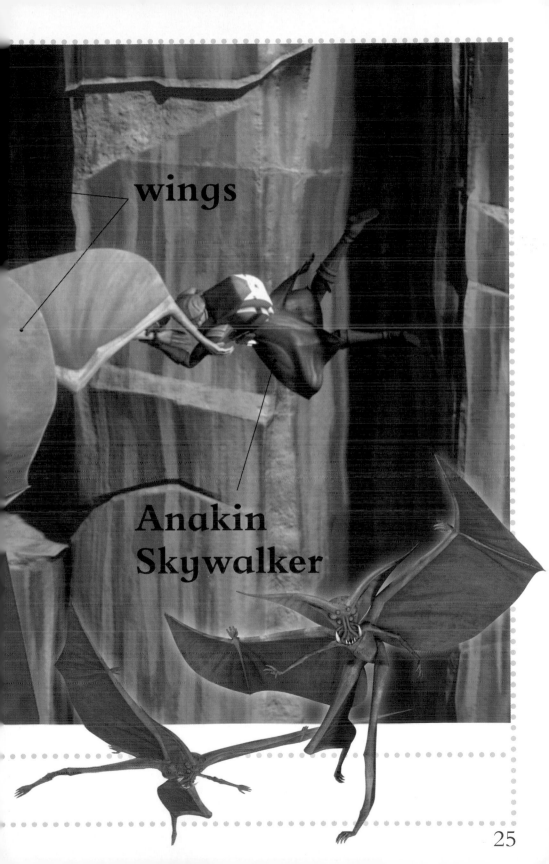

wings

Anakin
Skywalker

flying

aiwha (A-WAH)

Look at this massive aiwha. It can fly through the air.

swimming

Look at this
scary roggwart.
It has sharp claws
and robot arms.

robot arms

claws

roggwart (ROG-WORT)

Now you have met the creatures.

Which is your favorite?

Glossary

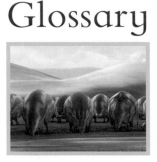

Herds
large groups of
animals

Marks
patterns on an
animal's skin

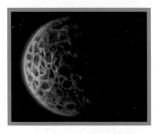

Moon
a small object that
goes around a planet

Spikes
pointed parts of
the body

Teeth
parts of the body that
are used to bite and
chew food